I HATE GEORGIA TECH
303 Reasons Why You Should, Too

Crane Hill
PUBLISHERS
BIRMINGHAM, ALABAMA
1995

I HATE GEORGIA TECH
303 Reasons Why You Should, Too

by Paul Finebaum

CRANE HILL PUBLISHERS

Copyright 1995 by Paul Finebaum

All rights reserved
Printed in the United States of America
Published by Crane Hill Publishers

Library of Congress Cataloging-in-Publication Data

Finebaum, Paul, 1955-
  I hate Georgia Tech: 303 reasons why you should, too / by Paul Finebaum. -- 1st ed.
    p.   cm.
  ISBN 1-881548-54-6
  1. Georgia Institute of Technology--Football--Miscellanea.
2. Georgia Tech Yellow Jackets (Football team). -- Miscellanea.
I. Title.
GV958.G43F56   1995
796.332'63'09758--dc20   95-39079
                                                              CIP

10   9   8   7   6   5   4   3   2   1

I HATE GEORGIA TECH

I Hate Georgia Tech Because…

1. When Bill Curry coached at Georgia Tech, fans considered changing the fight song from "The Rambling Wreck" to "The Rambling Idiot."

2. Most fans think MARTA is driven by a Georgia Tech Engineer.

3. George P. Burdell, the mythical student, could have started on the 1994 team.

4. A survey of 75,000 Atlanta residents revealed that 90 percent believed Georgia Tech was a private school. This result was largely attributed to the fact that the football team plays like one.

5. The remaining 10 percent did not know Georgia Tech had a football team.

6. What Atlanta tradition do Georgia Tech, the Atlanta Falcons, and the Atlanta Braves share? Once they make it to the finals, they choke.

7. Georgia Tech alumni like to brag that Bobby Dodd/Grant Field Stadium has one of the NCAA's largest press boxes. Considering those seats are the only ones occupied during home games, that was probably a wise decision.

8. Someday it will be revealed that Bobby Cremins, Newt Gingrich, and Phil Donahue were triplets separated at birth.

9. What do former coaches Bill Fulcher and Bill Lewis have in common? They both coached two years too many.

10. Atlanta residents believe *Revenge of the Nerds* was filmed on the Georgia Tech campus.

11. A good-looking Tech coed is obviously a visitor.

12. Even Divine Brown wouldn't work the corner of North Avenue and Techwood Drive.

13. Tech decided to host a Pee Wee Herman look-alike contest. Eighty-five percent of the male student population qualified.

14. Coca-Cola may be the most popular product in Atlanta, but on Tech's campus it's another form of coke.

15. Tech students enjoy the proximity to the High Museum.

16. The Georgia Tech School of Architecture has a class titled "Building with Legos."

17. Most fans believe Buzz should be given a high dosage of Ritalin and sent home.

18. Those same fans believe that if Buzz were unmasked they would find Jimmy Carter.

19. Sam Nunn graduated from Tech–need we say more?

20. To get votes from right-wing voters in Atlanta, Sam Nunn promised to eat the lunches of underprivileged school children.

21. Bill Curry is living proof you don't need a three-digit I.Q. to graduate from Georgia Tech.

22. Bill Curry's greatest contribution to the Georgia Tech football program was leaving.

23. Yellow Jacket fans believe a racist is someone who runs the Peachtree Road Race.

24. Some fans think Al Ciraldo should call the Super Bowl.

25. The good thing about Georgia Tech football games is there are always plenty of seats available.

26. The Georgia Tech campus would make a nice nuclear waste dump.

27. The fact that Bobby Dodd/Grant Field Stadium seats 46,000 proves how little there is to do in Atlanta.

28. Sam Nunn sleeps in the traditional gold-colored rat cap.

29. The most popular contraceptive used by Georgia Tech students: the pocket pen protector.

30. Some Tech coeds think intercourse is time off between classes.

31. Georgia Tech fans showed their class when they threw whiskey bottles at Coach Bear Bryant.

32. A better way to describe Tech fans having class: drop the first two letters of the word.

33. Bobby Cremins would have been better off had he stayed in South Carolina.

34. Georgia Tech decided to break from the SEC because they were afraid of the dirty word "competition."

35. The 1997 Georgia Tech homecoming game will most likely be played against Brenau Women's College.

36. Al Ciraldo is so old that when he was a teenager, the Dead Sea was still alive.

37. The Top 5 reasons students chose to attend Georgia Tech: Georgia was full.

38. They wanted to go to a school that didn't play major college football.

39. Their parents didn't want them to be distracted by watching the football team on national television.

40. Wanted to attend a school where they wouldn't have to wait in line for football tickets.

41. Wanted to attend a school where they wouldn't be intimidated by good-looking students.

42. Coach Bobby Dodd didn't always have Coke in his cup.

43. Hosea Williams is a Georgia Tech fan.

44. The *Atlanta Journal Constitution* would be a better paper without Mark Bradley.

45. Best form of birth control for a Georgia Tech coed: nudity.

46. Top 10 things Georgia Tech students do on a Friday Night: Drive around the perimeter.

47. Go out in Buckhead and get beaten up by a Georgia student.

48. Go out in Buckhead and get beaten up by a West Georgia student.

49. Go out in Buckhead and get beaten up by a high school student.

50. Go to Six Flags and calculate the time and velocity of each ride.

51. Drive to Gainesville and hang out in front of the dorms at Brenau Women's College.

52. Get beaten up by a Brenau student.

53. Try to make a new friend in Grant Park.

54. Get beaten up in Grant Park.

55. Go to the hall party in your dorm.

56. Bobby Cox is teaching a course at Georgia Tech titled "How to handle a woman."

57. Georgia Tech graduates place their diplomas on their windshield so they are eligible for handicapped parking.

58. A diploma from Georgia Tech is about as valuable as Bobby Cox's autograph.

59. After visiting the Atlanta campus, Bill Clinton said "This is the only school where the mascot looks better than the coeds."

60. George O'Leary's waistline is the only thing larger than the national debt.

61. Coach O'Leary tells his players, "Practice begins when the little hand is on the four and the big hand is on the twelve."

62. Furman Bisher began his career as a reporter for the *National Enquirer.*

63. Bobby Cremins was asked to do a Geritol commercial until they found out he was too old.

64. Georgia Tech basketball players believe a fast-break is leaving a 7-11 without paying.

65. The top five choices for commencement speaker: Bobby Cox.

66. Jerry Glanville.

67. Lester Maddox.

68. Paul Finebaum.

69. Hosea Williams.

70. The stupid Rambling Wreck car that circles the field before the games.

71. The hotels are so bad near the Tech campus that to get room service you have to dial 911.

72. There is something to be said for Coach O'Leary, and he is usually saying it.

73. The Tech campus doesn't need a Comedy Club. All students need to do for a laugh is look at the non-conference schedule in the ACC.

74. Bill Curry promised to turn the Tech program around quickly. He did so by taking the school from NCAA to oblivion in a short time.

75. Caning must be legal in Athens because the Yellow Jackets get beaten every year they play between the hedges.

76. A number of Tech fans are convinced Vince Dooley is related to Saddam Hussein.

77. Atlanta declared a national day of celebration when Bill Curry resigned from Georgia Tech.

78. Alumni believe a Rhodes Scholar is a student traveling down Techwood Drive.

79. The choice of car among Tech football players is a white Ford Bronco.

80. Tech students have petitioned to change the name of Atlanta's annual July 4th race to "The Peachtree Pot Race."

81. The FDA is considering allowing recordings of the *George O'Leary Show* to be used in place of sleeping pills.

82. Mark Furhman will be the guest of honor at the next spring game.

83. The Tech coaching staff had to separate Wives' Day and Girlfriends' Day because a couple of guys brought both.

84. Max Howell of WCNN has a mouth so big he can whisper in his own ear.

85. The best-selling book at the Tech campus bookstore this winter will be *I Hate Georgia.*

86. The second best-selling book will be *I Hate Paul Finebaum.*

87. The best-selling bumper sticker in Atlanta reads "Honk if you turned down the Georgia Tech coaching job."

88. More people turned down the Tech coaching job than turned down Pee Wee Herman for his senior prom.

89. Chris Morgan of WCNN is a poster child candidate for the "A mind is a terrible thing to waste" campaign.

90. When Fred Kalil's doctor told him recently to eat more vegetables, he started putting two olives in every martini.

91. Wes Durham is the kind of guy who goes to an orgy and complains about the cheese dip.

92. Kim King is so dull, when he goes to vote they hand him an absentee ballot.

93. Georgia Tech likes to brag it has one of the top engineering schools in America. Like somebody else would want one.

94. The only time Pepper Rodgers didn't run up the score was when he took the SAT.

95. The Tech business school offers a course titled "How to manage a Taco Bell."

96. The only time Coach George O'Leary is speechless is when somone asks him the last time he skipped a meal.

97. It's a good thing Tech fans don't have to pass an I.Q. test to become season-ticket holders.

98. Bobby Cox will be teaching a course next spring titled "How to beat up fans."

99. When basketball coach Bobby Cremins left Georgia Tech for South Carolina, the I.Q. of both places doubled.

100. Georgia Tech men refuse to marry kin unless they are at least third cousins.

101. Ludlow Porch never met a chili dog he didn't like.

102. Tech players always enjoy spring break to get away from Dave Kindred's column in the *Atlanta Journal-Constitution.*

103. Playboy featured a Varsity cook in its series "Girls of the ACC" because it couldn't find a good-looking Georgia Tech girl.

104. Coach George O'Leary contradicts himself and he is usually right.

105. Furman Bisher is fond of saying "I have no prejudices. I hate everyone equally."

106. Bobby Cremins once called Dr. Kevorkian after a loss to North Carolina.

107. The best-selling placard every year at the end of the Georgia game is "Wait until next year."

108. The food in the Tech campus restaurants is so bad the only card they accept is Blue Cross.

109. The captain of the Yellow Jacket cheerleading squad is determined by the girl with the smallest fever blister.

110. Bobby Cremins was once dropped as a member of the human race.

111. Georgia Tech fans won't visit Mount Rushmore because Bobby Dodd's face isn't featured.

112. If Al Ciraldo died during a football game, how would anyone know?

113. Coach Bobby Ross left Tech after several years complaining of illness and fatigue. The fans were sick and tired of him.

114. Coach Ross once said "Our society doesn't need to get rid of our coaches. Instead, we need to find away to get rid of our alumni."

115. Instead of using a driver's license for admission, graduates may now show their Mensa membership cards for entrance into Grant Field.

116. Some Tech coeds are so fat they have unlisted dress sizes.

117. Some Tech cheerleaders are so ugly they are often mistaken for circus animals.

118. After losing again to Georgia, coach Bob Lewis said "If lessons are learned in defeat, our team is getting a great education."

119. An academic All-American at Tech is someone who goes to class once a semester.

120. Bill Curry learned humility at Georgia Tech.

121. Tech has a graduate class titled "How to profit from the Olympics."

122. Coach O'Leary's brain was rejected by an organ bank.

123. A poll of Georgia Tech fans revealed they most wanted their sons to be like: Pee Wee Herman.

124. Kato Kaelin.

125. Ted Turner.

126. Ike Turner.

127. Sam Nunn.

128. Andrew Young.

129. Neil Young.

130. Jimmy Carter.

131. Billy Carter.

132. Newt Gingrich.

133. The Olympic Village's proximity to the Tech campus is ironic because you have the world's greatest winners next to the nation's greatest losers.

134. Coach O'Leary and his wife have made reservations for their summer vacation in the Olympic Village.

135. Tech graduates get lifetime memberships in Tupperware clubs.

136. Janet Reno was once captain of the Georgia Tech cheerleading squad.

137. Georgia Tech has a bowl tradition of staying home.

138. Like a broken-down horse, Bobby Cremins ought to be shot and put out of his misery.

140. Coach Ross is next in line for a brain transplant.

141. The worst profession in the state of Georgia is dentistry.

142. The best thing you can say about Georgia Tech is that it's not in Alabama.

143. Only 12 percent of Georgia Tech students have ever owned a bottle of shampoo.

144. The leaves begin to fall every autumn about the same time the Tech football program does.

145. Georgia Tech cheerleaders only have sex on days that end in "y."

146. Fans believe the television show *America's Most Wanted* was based on the Georgia Tech basketball team.

147. Delta Burke is a very, very big Georgia Tech fan.

148. There is something to be said for Rick Shaw of WGST, and he is usually saying it.

149. The men at Georgia Tech have so little understanding of pretty women that posters of Julia Child are often seen on dorm room walls.

150. The most feared words for any Georgia Tech cheerleader are, "Sorry, honey, we just ran out chili cheese dogs and onion rings."

151. Last year's homecoming queen was so ugly that when they took her to the State Capitol she was attacked by a plane.

152. The only thing that could make the Georgia Tech basketball team happier than winning the national championship is if they made marijuana legal.

153. Before declaring a major, freshmen at Tech are required to declare which is their favorite ride at Six Flags.

154. Dr. Gerald Wayne Clough is a dork.

155. The Georgia Tech liberal arts school has a foreign language requirement for in-state students: English.

156. Some Georgia Tech basketball players went ahead and enlisted last year instead of waiting for NBA draft day.

157. Bill Lewis once said, "The best thing about football is that it only takes four quarters to finish a fifth."

158. Coach Bobby Dodd was known to nap during the fourth quarter of big games.

159. It is a misdemeanor for Tech players to snort the chalk lines on the practice field.

160. Coach Brian Baker went swimming in Loch Ness and the monster got out.

161. The only thing more obnoxious than a Yellow Jacket fan is two Yellow Jacket fans.

162. The common belief by Tech alumni is that the ABC series *Coach* is based on the career of Pepper Rodgers.

163. What do you call it when the Tech football team has three players quit the team in one seven-day stretch? A good week.

164. In Poland they tell Georgia Tech jokes.

165. Georgia Tech is proud of its engineering program. Graduates get monogrammed pocket protectors at commencement.

166. The top 10 misconceptions about Tech engineering students: Women aren't prohibited from dating them; they just choose not to.

167. Beer really doesn't taste better through a straw.

168. Statistics are for losers.

169. Every student who doesn't take advanced calculus must take a semester of quantum physics.

170. Farm girls don't smell any worse than coeds who want to be engineers.

171. The weight room isn't a place to kill time before a dental appointment.

172. They can't write in their textbooks.

173. White socks and dark shoes will attract chicks.

174. Their degree will enable them to operate the Scream Machine.

175. Their degree will enable them to work in any theme park.

176. Tech's colors are gold and white, but after playing Georgia they are usually black and blue.

177. Tech sorority girls were disappointed to learn that talk of a hung jury in the O. J. Simpson case had nothing to do with some of the well-built jurors.

178. Georgia Tech brags about its large number of academic All-Americans. That just means their jocks understand exactly why they are losers.

179. Pick-up line heard at a local Tech bar: "For a fat girl, you really don't sweat much."

180. Georgia Tech girl's response: "Thanks!"

181. If it wasn't for pickpockets, Fred Kalil wouldn't have a sex life.

181. What do Georgia Tech girls make for dinner? Reservations.

182. Coach Bobby Ross said his fondest memory of the Tech campus was in his rearview mirror.

I HATE GEORGIA TECH

183. Coach Bill Lewis got the Tech job because he was the only candidate to spell his name right on the application.

184. They once tried to mate Tech cheerleaders with pigs. But there are some things even a pig won't do.

185. First place in a recent Tech radio giveaway was a pair of football season tickets.

186. Second place was two pairs of tickets.

187. Hugh Grant has been hired to escort prospective recruits to The Gold Club.

188. The Yellow Jackets want to play more football games at night. That way it wouldn't be just the players who were in the dark.

189. Tech's quarterback is believed to be color blind. What other explanation is there for always throwing the ball to the other team?

190. How can you have a first-rate school when it changes football coaches more often than some people change underwear?

191. The political science department has a special studies course that teaches the vice-presidents since Quayle.

192. Top 10 signs that you are a nerd: You are invited to a Georgia Tech fraternity party.

193. You are invited to a Georgia Tech sorority party.

194. When meeting someone new, your first response is "Can I see your Mensa card?"

195. You weigh less than your girlfriend.

196. You turn UGA red upon entering a Hooters restaurant.

I HATE GEORGIA TECH

197. If you have ever written an equation on a bathroom wall.

198. Driving the speed limit on I-285.

199. Your belt could also serve as a bra.

200. You are embarrased to order a naked dog at the Varsity.

201. You wear anything gold and black with a monogrammed yellow jacket.

202. What do you call a Tech graduate who gets married? Lucky.

203. What do you call the person who marries a Tech graduate? Challenged.

204. Georgia Tech football is about exciting as Bass fishing on Lake Lanier.

205. George P. Burdell was the first recipient of the Bobby Dodd Scholarship.

206. The legendary Coach John Heisman led the team to their first national championship in 1917, but people thought he was the Georgia coach because the seamstress forgot to sew the word Tech on the 1917 uniforms.

207. The Georgia Tech halftime show has been featured on *America's Funniest Home Videos.*

208. Coach Bill Lewis took the worst defense in the ACC and made it the worst in the country.

209. Tech students know they're drunk when they get sick in the stands and it's still not as disgusting as what's happening on the field.

210. Georgia Tech is the biggest joke in the ACC.

211. Steve Hummer is next in line for a brain transplant.

212. An earthquake ripped through Atlanta during a homecoming football game, totally destroying the seats in the student section at Bobby Dodd/Grant Field Stadium. Fortunately no one was injured.

213. Former coach Bill Curry is the biggest jerk to pass through Atlanta.

214. Or the state of Georgia.

215. Or for that matter, the entire universe.

216. In the dictionary next to the word "sleaze-bag" is the executive committee of the Georgia Tech Alumni Association.

217. O. J. Simpson could have gone to Atlanta after he escaped from the police because no one would have thought to look for a football player there.

218. The most popular class last semester at Tech was "How to install a screen saver."

219. Guessing the "Final Jeopardy" question is a requirment for admission to the Georgia Tech School of Engineering.

220. A good season at Georgia Tech is not being investigated by the NCAA.

221. The number one cologne used by Tech players is Ben-Gay.

222. It was discovered that the legendary "Wrong Way Riegels" was overheard asking coach William Alexander, "Now do I run away from my big toe or toward it?"

223. The only score Eddie Lee Ivery didn't run up was his SAT score.

224. The Tech golf team has had trouble in recent years trying to stay out of hazards—and that's before they reach the course.

225. The Georgia Tech quarterback recently took the homecoming queen to a dog show and she won.

226. Tech is proud to have natural grass return to Grant Field this year. But students have been using it all along.

227. Tech football players smoke so much grass, they have to get their stomachs mowed once a week.

228. The main concern regarding the installation of a real grass playing field is how to keep the Tech cheerleaders from grazing on the field.

229. Bobby Dodd would roll over in his grave if he could see some of the coaches currently employed on campus.

230. Coach O'Leary believes "Planet Reebok" is the planet right before Pluto.

231. Following is a list of the most hated sportswriters by Georgia Tech football fans: Tony Barnhart.

232. Mark Bradley.

233. Furman Bisher.

234. Paul Finebaum.

235. Steve Hummer.

236. Dave Kindred.

237. Ed Shearer.

238. Tim Tucker.

239. Scott Reid.

240. Norman Arey.

241. Bill Lewis had difficulty making enemies at Tech because his friends hated him so much.

242. Some fans believe a bong is not an instrument for drug use, but the sound of two quarterbacks colliding.

243. Pepper Rodgers once yelled at his team during halftime of a Georgia game "What's wrong with you guys? You're playing like a bunch of amateurs!"

244. The captain of the Georgia Tech cheerleading squad made the band in high school.

245. She also made the football and basketball team.

246. Visiting the Georgia Tech campus is like attending a Star Trek convention.

247. Popular saying by UGA football players: "A tie is like kissing a Tech girl."

248. The only good thing about Tech is that since nobody knows where it is, few people get to see what a dump it is.

249. The captain of the Tech cheerleading squad recently had her home phone number posted on the men's room of the athletic dorm.

250. The hooker who works on Techwood Drive is a virgin.

251. If Bobby Cremins had been captain of the *Titanic*, he would have told the passengers they were just stopping for ice.

252. Football games at Grant Field are so boring that pigeons fly into the broadcast booth and think the announcers are statues.

253. Al Ciraldo's favorite expression: "The past isn't what it used to be."

254. They can't start Happy Hour in Atlanta until sportswriter Mark Bradley leaves the room.

255. The favorite television show at the athletic dorm is the *Ricki Lake Show*.

256. Tech football players think Dr. Kevorkian is the team doctor.

257. A list of the 10 most admired women by Tech sorority members: Dr. Ruth.

258. Paula Jones.

259. Connie Chung.

260. Heidi Fleiss.

261. Lorena Bobbitt.

262. Divine Brown.

263. Tonya Harding.

264. Ricki Lake.

265. Susan Smith.

266. Gennifer Flowers.

267. Tech has considered changing their official fight song to "Where in the Heck is the Rambling Wreck?"

268. Football players have quit using blocking dummies and replaced them with cadavers for better simulation.

269. Fans are no longer allowed to bring cellular phones into the stadium because 911 was dialed too many times after Tech plays were made.

270. In football there are three seasons: bad, worse, and Tech season.

271. Some Tech cornerbacks confuse the term "nickel-back" with "nickel-bag."

272. Some Tech cheerleaders are so ugly they have to get prescription bathing suits.

273. The only sure thing in life is that Tech won't win the ACC.

274. The political science department has a special studies course that teaches the leaders of the KKK since David Duke.

275. Much like Forrest Gump, Bill Curry chose Alabama over Georgia Tech.

276. Pepper Rogers said, "Getting fired is tough enough. But being replaced by Bill Curry is like coming home from a long weekend and finding out your wife ran off with Don Knotts."

277. If it weren't for the classrooms, Tech would make a nice laboratory.

278. Tech players can do practically everything with a basketball but sign it.

279. Buzz is the dumbest mascot in the ACC.

280. The Homer Rice Center for Sports Performance is a nice location for a new stadium.

281. Bobby Harper and Art Eckman are so slow, they think Jenny Craig was a former Tech homecoming queen.

282. Notre Dame legend Knute Rnocke once said about former head coach William Alexander, "He gets more out of less than any coach in America." I bet he would rephrase that if he had seen former coach Bill Curry.

283. The captain of the Yellow Jacket cheerleading team was voted most likely to conceive.

284. Some Tech coeds don't shave under their arms.

285. The girls who don't shave under their arms are the most popular with the architecture students.

286. The engineering school offers a course called "How to avoid sex after marriage."

287. Georgia Tech fans consider a license plate personalized if it's made by a former Yellow Jacket player in prison.

288. A press guide is someone who helps the media find Georgia Tech's campus.

289. What do Tech engineering students and football players have in common? Neither know how to score.

290. After testing Buzz's I.Q. it is believed that Bill Curry could in fact be his father.

291. Fans think two people have walked on water, and one of them coached at Georgia Tech.

292. The athletic department claims that B.C. means "Before Curry."

293. The student newspaper *The Technique* can be found in the bottoms of bird cages throughout Atlanta.

294. Some Atlanta residents believe the Georgia Institute of Technology should be moved to Milledgeville, Georgia.

295. Other residents believe the majority of students transferred from Milledgeville.

296. The people who watch the Georgia Tech homecoming parade are generally referred to as "rubberneckers."

297. Tech students are angry that their annual Mini 500 Tricycle Race will not be included in the 1996 Olympic games.

298. Watching Tech football is like watching the second half of the 1994 baseball season.

299. And it draws about the same size crowd.

300. Georgia Tech is listed twice in the *Guiness Book of World Records*, once for their 220-0 wipeout score in the 1916 game against Cumberland College and second for having the world's largest nerd population.

301. Some students think coach Bill Lewis left because he wasn't allowed to participate in the Freshman Cake Race during homecoming festivities.

302. Some fans believe Bobby Cremins got the Dream Team assistant coaching job because he called so many games in his sleep.

303. Some Tech football team members will be competing in the 1996 Special Olympics.